KT-408-471

**Elaine Rockley**
Age 7

To Momtom,
who is still, yes *still,*
the most treasured
and loved mother
in the whole wide world.

Third edition published simultaneously in 1997
by Exley Publications in Great Britain and
Exley Giftbooks in the USA.

12 11 10 9 8 7 6 5 4

Second edition published in Great Britain in 1990
by Exley Publications.
Second edition published in the USA in 1992
by Exley Giftbooks.
First edition published in Great Britain
in 1976, revised and updated 1981.

ISBN 1-85015-839-8


Front cover illustration by Douglas Young, age 5
Back cover illustration by Adam Hadley, age 5

Typeset by Delta, Watford, Herts.
Printed and bound in China.

Exley Publications Ltd, 16 Chalk Hill, Watford,
Herts WD1 4BN, United Kingdom.
Exley Publications LLC, 232 Madison Avenue,
Suite 1206, NY 10016, USA.

*Other books in the series*
**Happy Birthday!**
(you poor old wreck)
**Grandmas and Grandpas**
(you lovable old dears)
**To Dad** (you poor old wreck

PRINTING HISTORY
**First edition** 1976
Thirteenth printing 1988

**Second edition** 1990
Fifth printing 1993

# To Mum
## (the kindest of ladies)

Mothers, mothers, young and old alike,
are still as sweet as ever.
**Patricia Lentong**

Mothers are incredible. And the people who say so most loudly and clearly are their children. Mums are funny. They have odd habits. They're endearing. But above all, they love their kids irrationally and beyond reason.

The entries in TO MUM are all absolutely genuine – the words, the pictures and the often hilarious spelling mistakes. There is no doubting the message of love that comes across. Again and again children tell of the times their mothers stay up half the night to care for them, of the way they trust their mothers, and can confide in them. They also, albeit guiltily, pay tribute to the immense amount of work mothers do for them, which is so often taken for granted.

First published twenty-one years ago TO MUM has been revised three times with added entries, new colour pictures and a new design. It is great fun to reissue this charming and innocent collection, and to watch the changes in the lives of mothers and their families.

Most mothers are now working, yet still somehow managing to support their children practically and emotionally. So much has changed, but the love and laughter are very much alive.

We hope this little giftbook will help a lot of children to say "I love you" and "Thank you" to their own special mother.

*Richard & Helen Exley*

# What is a mother?

Mums are walls which protect their children from the outside world.

**Adrian Leto** *Age 11*

Moms are the people who tell you to put boots on when it is raining, that you need a coat on in a heatwave and that you're still too young to have the radio-control robot that you've wanted since you were three.

**William**

A mother is someone to wake you too early and make you go to bed too early, and some one to see that you always do your piano practice.

**Susan** *Age 11*

A mother is a woman who buys you chocolates and when you have fillings at the dentist she blames you.

**Aishling**

Mother is a working wife, busy all the day, Shopping in her lunch hour, running all the way.

**Linda Parkinson** *Age 15*

# A mother is supposed to love you and wash boys' smelly socks

**Sally Arthy**

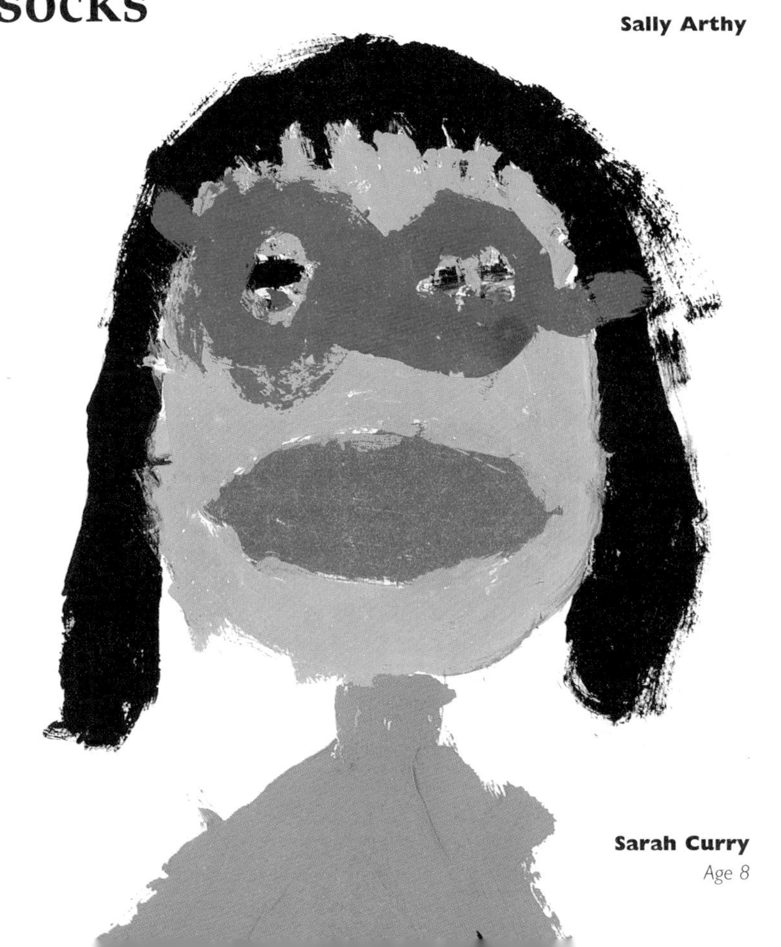

**Sarah Curry**
*Age 8*

A mum is a woman who says "go to bed" and when she says that, you stay very quite and she forgets about you.

**Aishling Nolan**

A mother is a person who looks after you if you get scared, and if you want your teddy bear.

**Elizabeth Bird** *Age 8*

Mothers drive you ten times round town on Sunday, looking for funny chimneys to report to the teacher.

**Timothy Robinson** *Age 12*

Mothers are people who are angry when you're at home and sad when you're away.

**Vinay** *Age 12*

A mum is someone who always asks you to do something when you're just about to do something else.

**Genevieve**

Moms wash and dry any dirty football uniforms, five minutes before going to school, having only been given them that morning.

**Michael Haworth-Maden** *Age 12*

A mother is not a proper mother if she does not watch a soap two or three times a week.

**Andrew** *Age 13*

A mother is someone who sings in the kitchen.

**Elisabeth Fenton** *Age 12*

**Daniel Griffiths John** *Age 8*

Mothers are like
volcanoes
About muddy puddles
on the floor.
ke prehistoric monsters
Like cars screaching
On a wet morning.
Mothers have to be in
a hurry
When the door bell goes
The telephone rings
The baby cries
They all start at once.
Some mothers get in a rage
Rushing all over the place
My mother does.

**Philip** *Age 7*

**Amanda Gray** *Age 8*

# Multi-purpose mamas

To a toddler, a mother is an explorer, an astronaut, an indian chief, a cowboy... anything that he thinks of as a game. To an infant, she is a helper, confider, a comforter, even a protector.

When she listens to a junior she always understands and she is always there to tell worries to.

**Alison Bain**

A mother is a helper
A finder of lost things
A pocket money giver
An angel without wings.

**Laura Dalgleish** *Age 8*

# God created mother because he could not be present everywhere.

**Taniya Sharma** *Age 15*

# If it was not for mothers we would look like a sack of potatoes.

**Tony Martin** *Age 12*

Without a
mother the
family would
always be
fighting and
never be
lunch on
time


**Jane Moppel** *Age 12*

# Life without her

To all mums everywhere, what would we do without you? Who would do our cleaning and cooking? I certainly wouldn't do it all. What! Wash smelly socks and grubby shirts. Burn my hands in hot, fatty, soapy water, no fear!

**Lisa Ollard** *Age 13*

**Jacob Thornton** *Age 6*

If I had not got a mother my bed would not be done and I would be staying up late watching television. I would all ways be spending my money on things that I would not need. My dinners would probably be a tin of Coke and a cold sandwich and no one would be able to take me out in the car. I would have to do all the house work and so I would not have any spare time. At school I would be a little Dracula and so no one would like me. So I am glad to have one.

**Michael Jenkins** *Age 10*

# In tribute

It is lovely to have a mam. Mams are lovely people and I am going to be a lovely mother when I grow up. I am going to care for my children like my parents cared for me.

**Estelle Moreton**

The things my mum does for me are uncountible. She has been helping me hours on end ever since I was born.

**Mark Lewis** *Age 8*

**She laughs when I laugh, she cries when I cry, she lives when I live. I can't say more about her except that she lives for me and I live for her.**

**Josephides Panayiota** *Age 16*

Mothers
do not die
because
they live in
the hearts of
their children


**Berna Tahmiscioglu** *Age 16*

**Susan Holliday** *Age 7*

# Funny old thing

The way she worries about my school tests anyone would think she was taking them not me.

**Robert Booth** Age 12

When my mammy talks on the telephone she talks posh.

**Hilary** Age 7

My mum likes watching old fogies' things on television, but she's kind and that is all that matters.

**Rachel** Age 11

My mommy calls me her little tweedy-twer-heart and my sister her goosy.

**Clare Aldridge**

# Silly billies!

They're really delightful things, always the best in the world, although quite often very silly things.

**Stephen**

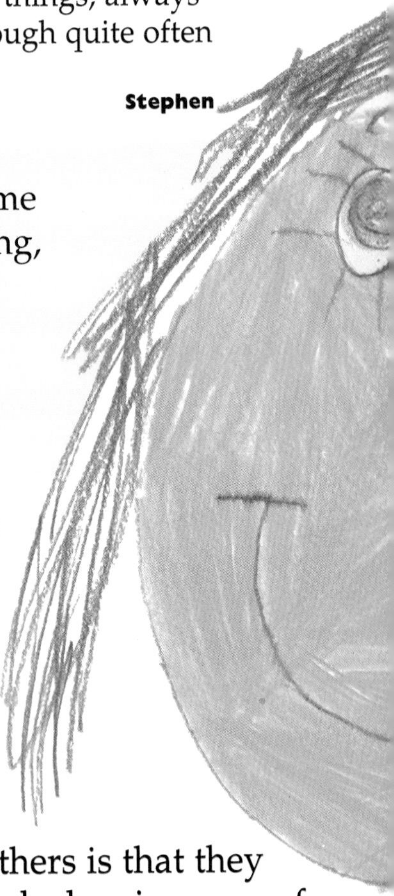

Truely most of the time
Ma is a lovable old thing,
although she has got a
knack for breaking
plates, cups etc.
quite a lot.

**Jane** *Age 13*

My mommy gets me
nuts because she once
put butter in the
washing machine
instead of washing
powder.

**Tracey** *Age 8*

The trouble with mothers is that they don't play games though she gives me a few rotten under arm rolls in the summer after school.

**John** *Age 1C*

Adam Hadley Age 5

Ma's like a football. She gets knocked araund a bit but always the same shape.

Mark Age 11

Adele Cox Age 9

**Jessica Goul**

# Do you know I was born because I wanted to be near my mommy?

**Claudia Martinez** Age 8

# Ma and me

She is kind and gentle. Sometimes my mother really loves me and she looks at my face and she smiles at me. I go and sit by her.

**Balbinder Kaur Kalsi** *Age 11*

Sometimes Mother is angry. But sometimes it's NOT my fault I get angry and fight back. Mum yells and so do I. But in the night, when everything is still, and I am still awake, I hear mum come in, she whispers that she always has and always will Love me. That is the best part. But she never knows that I am awake, And as sleep overtakes me, I feel, Happy, And Loved....

**Vandana Tandon** *Age 10*

**Jennifer Mary Bromley** *Age 5*

# Isn't she a pain. . .

Mothers are the sort of people who, before a western starts in the evening, send you to bed saying how awful it will be and then wake you up saying what a fantastic show it was.

**Nicholas**

I don't like the way she puts me to bed. When I am wide awake at night. she makes me go to sleep, and when I'm fast asleep in the morning, she makes me get up!

**Stephen**

Mommy tidys up our rooms and throws my teddy's head away.

**Steven**

**John** *Age 9*

**Ian**

The habit no mum should be without is nattering on the phone; no mother would be complete without it.

**Miles Hutchinson** *Age 10*

# Chatter, chatter

One thing mine can't stand is being stood out on the street gabbing away, she would much rather sit down and gab over a cup of coffee.

**Dave** Age 14

She is always natting on about her and her sister when she was small, I pretend to listen but I watch TV instead. We just say YEH, YEH, YEH. She soon shuts up

**Timothy**

She is always talking and the only time she is quiet is when she is very interested in what's on television and even then she puts in a quick comment. She is also quiet when she is asleep.

**Julie** Age 9

**Alice Nilsen Fehn** Age 7

# Going out

I think mine is funny because when she plans to go out she has to do her hair, her face and by the time she has finished, it is to late to go out.

**Ean** *Age 10*

Every time Mommy goes out to a dance she puts her false nails on, and she looks ever so funny, and Daddy puts aftershave on, and he smells as well.

**Elisabeth** *Age 7*

My mother powders her face,
Puts lipstick on,
And cover herself in perfume,
That's why my father disowns her at parties.

**Sophia** *Age 11*

**Andrea Scown** Age 7

# God didn't have enough arms for keeping kids out of trouble so he invented moms.

**Alice Lumpkin** *Age 11*

# The best thing I thought Ma did was having me, but others might not think so.

**Tim Tripp** *Age 12*

My mum has weird rules that I have to obey, like having a bath, keeping my bedroom tidy and even having my hair cut.

**Christopher Moates** *Age 12*

She says
I'm nicest when
I am asleep
because
I can not say
anything wrong.

**Richard** Age 12

**Philippa** Age 8

# A kind of civil war

Mums are vultures that hang over you, telling you that you have to clear the snow or make your bed. They nag at you, giving you lectures on life in general and how to make your bed in particular.

**Peter**

My mom smacks me when I am naughty it hurts me very much but I deserve it.

**Stephen** Age 9

Mothers make you go to the barbers as though you were going to a dog show.

**Peter Wilkinson** Age 11

Mom gets up at 7.30 am and begins her routine day of housework, headaches and yelling

**Mark** Age 13

She gets mad when all of us done something bad on the same day, and that's the time when you shouldn't bother her too much.

**Juanita**

Mommys are nice except when they find gum sticking to their carpet.

**Michelle** *Age 10*

She Sometimes gets mad and once She got So mad that She made us make our own Breakfast.

**Mark** *Age 9*

# In my mother's arms

My mother always has room for me in her arms. She's never too busy to give our family the special love a mother can only give.

**Donna Jauga** *Age 9*

My mother cares for me. I feel that I've got day and night protection when I'm near her.

**Martha van Kees** *Age 9*

She is the person you can come to for comfort, when all hope is lost, like an old teddy bear with one eye and half an ear.

**Patricia Bowie** *Age 13*

Moms are always busy but never too busy to give you a quick cuddle.

**Helen Rankin** *Age 9*

My mum is nice to sit on. She's nice and soft and bouncey.

**Paul Fanneaux** *Age 10*

**Hadas Nahari** Age 9

# My mother's hands

These hands lifted me when I was a baby. They dried away the tears when I cried at night or when I was upset. My first food came from her hands. She helped me tie my laces, hold the spoon in my hands, shampooed and bathed me. I remember the sadness I felt when I let go of her hands on my first day at school. Although they may get old and wrinkled I will always remember what those precious hands did for me.

**Sean McGilligam**

My mother's hands can be soft and hard. They are like smooth silk when she is rubbing my cheeks, and like hot fire when my mother is smacking me for being naughty. They do loving things like combing my hair cleaning my ears and taking care of my clothes. They do sweet things like making waffles and cakes. If I had to give my mother's hands a grade they would get a B+. If it wasn't for the spankings her hands would get a big "A".

**Kim Wilkinson**

She brushes my hair so it is not tangly.

**Teri Cothran** Age 6

# The comforter

A mom is a person who cares for you and tucks you in at night. When you've made a mistake she says it's quite allright. Someday you will have to grow out of this stage.

She doesn't want to let you out of her big lovable cage. When it's time to leave her and face the big wide world, Always remember: She is the one who cares and she will always shed the most tears.

**Jan Menno** Age 13

A mother is someone who comforts you. Because she misses you, even for one minute. Because you are her child.

**Kristin Thompson** Age 8

A mum is someone who always knows when there is something wrong even if you don't tell her.

**Lisa Tresa** Age 14

# Like a rose

My mother is medium sized, brown as a berry and as cool as a cucumber. Her hair is red and thick. She has a proud walk, and is as tender as a chicken. A rose is as beautiful as my mother, and she is as fresh as a daisy, and as strong as an ox. When I grow up I would like to be as beautiful as my mother. And have the beautiful ways she has. My mother is more precious than gold.

**Carmen Ramnath** *Age 11*

My mother is the coolest person in the world. Sometimes she looks like a rose and other times she is just a plain daisy. When she is a rose you can imagine that my mom is very nice.

**Wanda Michels** *Age 11*

**Abbas** *Age 8*

# Welcome!

She doesn't know how to cook very well but when she cooks the dinner it seems to have something special about it. When she makes my bed I think she puts something into it, and I don't awake all night.

**Conchita Rey Benayas** *Age 10*

**Brenel Menezes** *Age 9*

When I come home from school, who would be there to make a delicious, warm chocolate drink and maybe some hot muffins or a quick snack before having a proper dinner. I might have spaghetti bolognaise with a rich luscious pudding, oozing with cream and chocolate sprinkled carefully over the top. Or another night I might have ham and potato with salt and pepper laid over my potato, not forgetting to dribble the tomato sauce over everything. Only a nice, welcoming mother could do that, making things just how you like them.

**Lisa Ollard** *Age 13*

# She's always there

When you are ill who is always there,
Quietly sitting stroking your hair?
WHO is always waiting for you to come home?
WHO welcomes you with open arms?
WHO never lets you down?
WHO wakes you up with a lovely smile in the morning?
WHO's always ready to help?

**Vivienne Gilbert**

Some mothers' apron strings are never cut, just stretched.

**Patricia Sisti** *Age 14*

When all other friends have deserted you, your mother is always here.

**Catherine Woodall** *Age 14*

Imagine you are in a stone room with a metal door, metal roof, you are bolted off from the world. Mum is the key. If she is taken away it is nightmares and horrors if she is there it is dreams, treats and love and care if there were no Mums we would be nothing. Mums are the key to the future. Mums were put on earth to care and love not to rage and hate. Mums help us, guide us and love us. If there were no Mums no us would be there. Mums are to run to for comfort.

**Fiona Finch** *Age 8*

Always a friendly smile,
Always open arms
Willing to help while –
Troubles are at their worst.
The door is always open
To us their children.

**Alexandra Hitchings**

**Wendy** *Age 6*

# She's an old softie

## A mother is probably the most likley one to give in to you.

**Jessica** *Age 11*

A mother is someone to help you eat your food when you can't eat it all, so it looks like you ate it all.

**Teri Burns** *Age 11*

Even the roughest of mothers are very gentle and kind inside, or else they could not be mothers.

**Elaine Wong**

If I am naughty I always break it to my mom first.

**David** *Age 12*

My mum is a bit stupid because every time I ask for something she buy's it me.

**Debbie** *Age 10*

I have a super mother who makes cakes, puts them in the pantry and doesn't notice when I eat them.

**Mark Wickham-Jones** *Age 13*

A mum is sombody who always understands your feelings, special feelings, that only my mother and I will ever know about. A person you'll always remember, the rest of your life. My mum.

**Karen Angelini** *Age 10*

**Rupa** *Age 8*

# Take good care of her

Mothers deserve
a couple of surprises
and treats themselves,
for all the hard work
they do.

**Louise Twaite**

So love your mother
all you can,
While you have her now.
She wont be there
all your life,
So love her all you can.
with all you know how.

**Alison Baker** Age 7

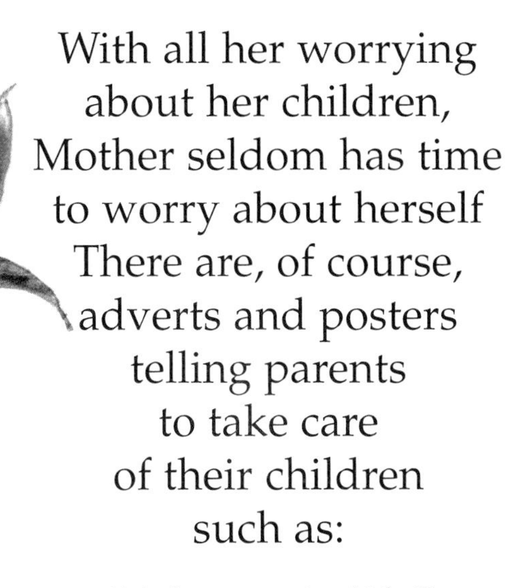

With all her worrying
about her children,
Mother seldom has time
to worry about herself
There are, of course,
adverts and posters
telling parents
to take care
of their children
such as:

"A lesson in life"
and
"Under your feet
is better than under a car."
So, why not
have posters saying:
"Take care of your mother,
she's valuable"
and
"Make sure your parents,
Clunk Click Every Trip."

**Alison Bain**

# My mam isn't really a beauty queen, but in my heart she is the prettiest woman in the world.

**Ian** Age 1C

# Beautiful in her own way

My mom is as beautiful
as anyone can be,
well maybe not to everyone
but always to me.
Now I don't mean always
by looks because you learn
all that junk from T.V.
and books. But I mean that she
has a beauty inside.

**Donna Nitte** Age 12

My mum's, well, she's beautiful in her own way. She's not exactly a beauty queen, but you can't just go and draw a picture of her and say "That's my mother". There's something about her, whether it's her willingness to listen or what I don't know. But I'm glad she's mine.

**Daryl Mitchell**

# Poor working mothers!

*My mother is very patient. She would have to be with five kids, four dogs and two jobs*

**Pam Repec** *Age 12*

My mother gets up between six and half past am and she does some general housework and makes breakfast. At seven she wakes up my two brothers and they all have breakfast. Then Mammy gets the boys ready for school, wakes up Daddy, and at quarter to eight she goes off to work.

**Joanna Blake** *Age 11*

My mum she works so very hard.
She must be near to tears,
Cos' gimie, gimie! More, More!
Are the only words she hears.

**Susan Harvie** *Age 10*

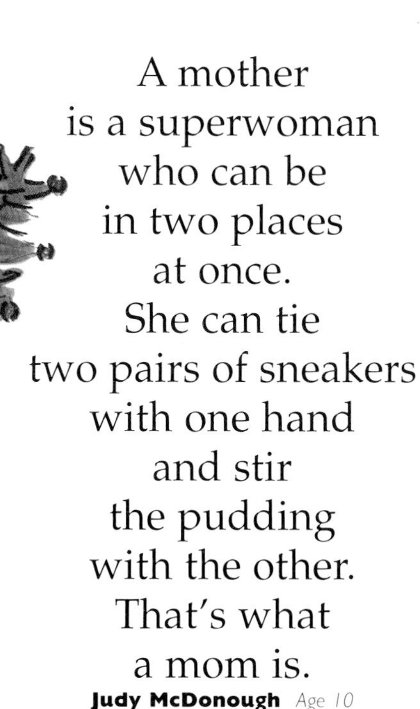

A mother
is a superwoman
who can be
in two places
at once.
She can tie
two pairs of sneakers
with one hand
and stir
the pudding
with the other.
That's what
a mom is.

**Judy McDonough** *Age 10*

They say "A mother's place is in the home", but mine doesn't think so.

**Leroy** *Age 11*

**Maxine Howitt** *Age 10*

# A slave to her family

My mom is so busy she has not got any hobbies I suppose her hobbey is cleaning the house.

**Craig** Age 9

Be nice to your mother. Don't let her be your work horse, will you?

**Donald Ryan** Age 8

I sometimes think that they are bossy and and tempered but when I think about it I realise how hard it is to be a mother. It is make breakfast, wash up, go shopping, cook, wash up, type, meet the school bus, cook, wash, type. I can see why they ask you to wash up or get your own food. I begin to wonder why they ever become mothers in the first place.

**Alan** Age 15

A mother is not just a mother, she is a Human Being too.

**Barbara Allbritton** *Age 11*

## Who would want to be a mother?

Everyday you clean the house listening to love songs on the radio while you sweep, dust and polish, making our beds, scorching your hands in the washing up, or trying to make the old washing machine work. When all the cleaning's done you can have a rest with a snack and last month's paper which you still have not read. Then there is the shopping and hurry to meet the school bus. Homework comes next. "Mommy how do you do this?" or "Mommy how do you do that?". After supper, Dallas comes on, but of course you have to do the washing up, type more letters, or sew buttons on the school shirts. When she has finished all she is fit for is bed. Perhaps I do not really want to be a mother after all.

**Susan**

# Thank you

My mother is so kind
I do not know how to thank her.
How can I thank you
my Mommy?

**David Webb** *Age 9*

Mother, at every difficult moment in my life
I turn to you. You are the only person who can
help me whenever I need
help, the only person who
can make a sacrifice for me.
That will be understood
only by children who
have lost their mothers.

**Savva Evangelia** *Age 17*

Mother, I will remember
your sweet face for ever.
Never will I forget
anything you did for me.

**Savva Evangelia** *Age 17*

**Caroline de Silva** *Age 9*

*"Thank you, Mother."*
It isn't easy to express the things I want to say, For what goes on unnoticed, every single day. But still you are there, with all your understanding heart And those never-to-be-forgotten words of advice.

**Jesse O'Neill** *Age 13*

**Iris Harcel**

Who do you go to when
You're in a mess?
Who do you turn to when
You're in distress?
Remember her birthday
And Mother's Day too
You look after her
And she'll look after you!

**Debbie Russell** *Age 16*

# Lessons in life

A good mother is worth a hundred teachers. The teacher teaches lessons from books while the good mother teaches everything that is useful in life.

**Mona Fouad El Sakka** *Age 16*

She told me that I must learn to be kind, to be a good friend, and always to be ready to help. But I think the most important thing I learnt was to trust myself. It gave me a lot of confidence. My parents gave me the basic values I needed, and because they taught me how to learn, I learnt all the other things by myself And for that I thank them and love them.

**Michal Arlosoroff** *Age 17*

And as I grew she shared good times with me. She taught me to be realistic and understanding, she taught me how a mother should be, but most importantly, she taught me how to be a woman.

**Debra Duel** *Age 15*

**Sarah Eyule** Age 7½

My mother means morning
A beautiful
morning

**Abby** Age

**Claire Mullan** Age 9

Mums are really groovey.
Helping us when we are sick.
Washing, drying, all the lot.
They are hard working ladies
busy here, busy there, busy
nearly everywhere.

**Ruth Shaw**

Mother... That was the first
word that I learned when I
was little. And she was the
first person I knew and loved.

**Berna Tahmiscioglu** Age 16

Mothers have a heart with a key. they open it and love pours out

**Marcia** Age 9

A mother's worry
never ends for her children.

**Sheryl A. Hartley** Age 12

"Mum" is the only word that makes everybody all over the world happy, the symbol of devotion. She gives everything that she has, sometimes even her life, for her children without hesitating a moment.

**Hasan Ali Tolgay** Age 17

# A mother is. . .

A mother is someone who has to wash faces and count heads when she's ready to go somewhere.

**Melonie Dixon** *Age 11*

Mothers are people who sit up worrying about you when you come home they holler at you.

**Gary Crees** *Age 13*

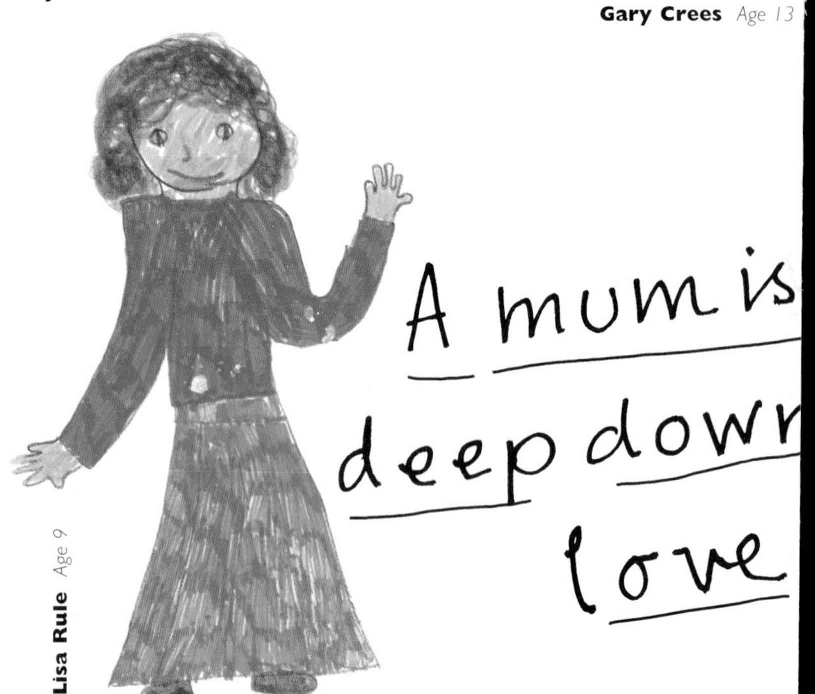


**Lisa Rule** *Age 9*

A mother is a loving angel. Between her arms you find warmth and love which you can never find anywhere else.

**Shahira Yossef** *Age 16*

A mum is a person who cries when you do something bad, and cries even harder when you do something good.

**Robin DiBiase** *Age 14*

when

there is

**Aldo A. Gomez** *Age 7*

**Sarah Cakebread** *Age 10*